SPILT MILK

Aisha Ali

ARCHWAY
PUBLISHING

Archway Publishing books may be ordered through booksellers or by contacting:

Archway Publishing
1663 Liberty Drive
Bloomington, IN 47403
www.archwaypublishing.com
1 (888) 242-5904

ISBN: 978-1-4808-8471-7 (sc)
ISBN: 978-1-4808-8472-4 (e)

Library of Congress Control Number: 2019917830

Print information available on the last page.

Archway Publishing rev. date: 12/5/2019

*To the one seeking a light on their
darkest days, this is for you.
To my family, who has supported me during my
darkest days, I couldn't have done it without you.
And to my late father, who was the catalyst for this
entire journey, I'm truly happy now thanks to you.*

Foreword

This book began as teardrops on torn pieces of paper during a time in my life when darkness had swallowed me whole. During those days, I was neither alive nor dead; I merely existed. After suffering a miscarriage and losing my beloved father within a week, followed by the passing of my loving aunt four months later, I began to question every aspect of my life.

My father asked me on his death bed, "Aisha, are you happy?" I remember responding hurriedly, "Yes, daddy. Please don't worry." But, was I? I can't recall ever asking myself that question. What is happiness? Am I *actually* happy? Do I deserve to be happy? Do I have the capacity to welcome happiness? And what must I do to prioritize my happiness? Once I began asking myself those questions, I felt as though I finally arose from a deep slumber that had incapacitated me for far too long. I finally removed the rose-coloured glasses I'd been wearing for five years, and for the first time in my life, I chose *myself* by seeking divorce. My father's words were unknowingly his last gift to me.

The pain of what I had endured over the course of five years and my current reality was so overwhelming that no words, no amount of ice cream, and no number of well-meaning people were able to soothe me. I was submerged. So, I did the only thing that I knew how to do: I began to write. And write. And write. I wrote every day without fail until I had no more words left to express. My written words were my saving grace, by the Will of God.

During the time following my personal tragedies, a multitude of people asked me the question, "How are you doing?" They were all seeking the same response, hoping to hear me say, "I'm okay," or "I'm doing well." And each time, without fail, I gave them the response that they desired to hear. However, behind my forced smile, I wished to say: "Actually, I'm not doing so well; I'm hurting a lot right now. I feel as though the earth has swallowed me whole, and I can't stop crying. But I know given some time, I will be okay."

But of course, that response would make others uncomfortable. So instead, I just smiled and repeated the same words robotically, wondering when the topic of pain became so taboo. I believe that the only thing pain proves is that you're *alive,* and willing to be *vulnerable* and truly *feel.* Since when was that something to be ashamed of? I know it's much easier to numb your feelings with comfort food, people, or substances; it's easier to choose not to feel–to no longer be human–than to be hurt again. I did that for five years, and for five years I suffered; I felt detached. So, I did the bravest thing anyone can do when heartbroken: I allowed myself to feel every emotion. That, too, was painful; but it passed.

Fast forward a year into this healing journey and I still can't say that I'm completely okay. However, I *can* say that I'm much better because of my willingness to face my feelings. I'm beginning to spend time with myself, and discover all the little things that make me who I am. It's an exhausting process, but I know that the work will eventually get easier. And I know with certainty that, given more time, I *will* be able to say that I'm okay.

If you've picked up this book with the intention of searching for a sliver of hope, I thank you. Thank you for opening your heart to me during a time when you wish to protect it most. I cannot guarantee that you'll find that hope here, but I can say that what you're looking for is already within you, and sometimes what you're searching for is someone to articulate it. I pray that I can be that someone, and I hope that after reading this book, you can return the favour and be someone else's "someone."

Peace and love,
Aisha Ali

Contents

Prologue
ME

My page is dry,
pen in hand.
Words are at the tip,
but why can't I write?
So many words left unsaid;
so many feelings ignored.
If I face it all
and begin to scribe it all,
can it be undone?
So, I wait
and wait.
Not knowing when I will overcome this.
Not knowing if I will ever begin.
But he is insistent,
forceful.
His words grip me by the shoulders
and shake,
      shake,
           shake,
                explode.

Chapter 1
TAINTED LOVE

In the beginning,
everything was different
with her.
The sky was bluer.
The water tasted better.
The cold was bearable.
And the little they had
was enough.
He doesn't remember
when it all changed.
He just remembers feeling
cold.

He had a smile that never
quite reached his eyes.
She peered into them and found herself
swimming in a darkness that was
neither calming
nor frightening.
He was a painter;
his velvety fingers were the
brushes that stained her body
with violet designs.
He was a rose with hidden thorns.
Her supple hands gave way
to a plethora of scars.
She should've known by the look in his eyes
that loving him would cause her to doubt
all that she knew about
love.
        The beginning of a painful story.

She was a spider,
creating a web of images,
depicting their future, promising
if he were to endure *just* a little more,
he could then have her love.
He could have it all.
But
he could never see past the flimsy silk
swaying in the wind.
He didn't tell her, though.
    The spider's home is the frailest of homes.

He was the sun when
they had first met.
She would bathe in his attention,
feeling his warmth envelope her.
But as the days became shorter,
his warmth began to recede into the night,
replaced by a biting frost that was
foreign to all those who knew him.
    He was her spring day turned winter's night.

She molded him into a vessel
and placed him atop a pedestal
in the dust-filled attic.
There he stayed
with only sadness to fill him.
Drip,
      drip,
            drip.
She only recalled his
existence when he could no
longer contain it within himself.
Up she waltzed,
dusted him off
and poured him out,
only for it to be repeated
again and again.
      The cycle of abuse.

She tried to imagine their life
in a year's time,
but all she saw was herself
rooted in front of a blank canvas,
paintbrush mounted on the easel,
a rainbow of colors neatly arranged in her palm,
untouched,
as if her future were on standby,
waiting for her to take control—
to pick up the paintbrush
and paint.
    There was no tomorrow with him.

His memory begins to falter.
Why can't he recall
his own words?
Her eloquent speech
casts him under her
spell.
"Yes, you're right."
He nods.
"Yes, I did say that,"
he agrees,
despite the heavy knot
in his tongue.
Sometimes,
he wishes he could escape
her spell.
Sometimes,
he wishes he could disappear.
    Spellbound.

Often times,
it is the loving hands that
cause the most pain.
She later realized
that they weren't so loving
after all.
    Deception.

He stopped believing in love
at a young age;
instead, he believed in usefulness
because that seemed to be
the only reason why
others kept him around.
So, when he was in his twenties
and she finally uttered those three words
intending to use him for a little longer,
he told her,
"You do not love me;
you love all that I do for you."
    Transparent.

Chapter 2
TRAPPED

Deliberate defiance and
disrespectful decisions.
Why is he the agony that ripples through her body?
Chills run down her spine each time she sees him,
but that doesn't stop him from coming near.
What will stop him?
What will make him end his tyranny?
All she wishes is to be free,
to be rid of the shackles he has placed on her.
She wishes to collect the pieces of her heart
that he broke with his 'loving' hands.
She wishes to put the pieces back together,
but she can only do that if today is the end—
if today is goodbye.
She needs to stand in her call to prayer,
feel the wind in her hair,
and smell the salty fragrance of the sea.
Only then will his reign end.
Only then will she be
free.

Each time he overcomes one hurdle,
two more appear.
He finally cries for help,
but her charming mask overpowers
the truth.
It never gets easier,
just becomes a different type of
difficult.

In a culture that values her brothers' hunger more than her own,
that teaches her to wash their clothes
and cook their food in the absence of their mother,
she saw it coming.

The elders strolled into her home,
unapologetically unannounced
to instruct her to be patient,
sacrifice,
before she could part her lips in greeting.
She saw it coming.

Those words are often beaten into the women
who are suffering the most.
"That's normal;
all men do that.
Don't destroy your family."
As if his actions did not bring her to her knees
and break her resolve to live a thousand times over.
As if her gathering the strength to stand up
for the first time
is a crime.
She saw it coming.

"Be patient; sacrifice,"
they repeated one last time.
She then realized that it's easier
to suppress your humanity
than to change generations of accepted indifference.
        Trapped in a man's world.

I wonder,
do you see her?
Do you see what her eyes contain,
or do you just see the smile plastered onto
her thinning face?
Do you see the scars that trace her body,
or do you just see the rich melanin that conceals the pain?
Do you love her for who she truly is,
or do you just love her for who she pretends to be?
I wonder,
are you willing to question all that you see,
or is the truth too burdensome for you to carry?
Ignorance is bliss.

In,
       out.
In,
       out.

He focuses on
breathing,
the only thing
he can control.

In,
       out.
In,
       out.
       Repeat.

Trust is a strength
only unharmed people
possess,
because how
can one who's been burnt
by the very flames they believed
to bring them warmth
willingly out stretch their hand
once more?
"Trust that he'll change,
and embrace him in earnest,"
the elders instructed her.
But how can someone erase
the carvings on a stone?
Her young, wide-eyed self
accepted his words—the storyteller—
despite the unsettling image she saw.
She believed wholeheartedly,
blindly trusting the good that she heard
and so desperately wanted to be true.
But now,
she is skeptical,
fearful—
attempting to plug her ears
and widen her eyes
in order to judge
someone's actions
before their words.
    Jaded.

If they were to see
the marks her words
left on his soul,
they would have never
doubted his cries.
    It's not always physical.

The tears continue to fall,
like the way rain pours
in abundance,
seemingly out of nowhere.
Not knowing whether it'll be a light rain
or a rainstorm.
No silver lining in sight.

Is this
what it feels like
to lose all of
your hopes
and dreams?
     Empty.

She catches herself daydreaming often.
Perhaps it's an escape.
Regardless,
she continues to indulge.
　　Temporary happiness.

Who do you think he'd be
had he not gone through
those painful moments?
    Foolish curiosity.

Chapter 3
BREAKTHROUGH

Confusion consumes her.
Should she do it?
She was certain.
But now,
right now,
she no longer is.
Reality starts to set in—
all that she's about to lose.
Breaking away from the one
she imagined a life with.
Is she ready for that?
She's terrified.

Her young, doubtful self resurfacing.

Waves wash over him:
of guilt,
of sadness,
of relief,
of contentment.
If only the waves
were like drops of rain,
so if he carried an umbrella,
only his feet
would become
                    soaked.

Her heart has torn.
Her palms have weathered.
Her smile has faded.
Her eyes have darkened.
She stares into the mirror and wonders,
when will she see herself
again?
    Trying to find herself in her reflection.

When will the rain
bring growth?
When will the fire
bring warmth?
Until when will he
wait?
The fire continues to burn.
The rain continues to flood.
He continues to wait
for it all.
    Anticipating what may never come.

She longs for the day
that her love will be returned
just as wholeheartedly
as it was given.
    Still waiting.

He's been avoiding you.
Busying himself to prevent thoughts
of you.
Nevertheless,
here you are.
A heavy cloud looming overhead
that will inevitably pour forth
its containment.
Its temporary darkness brings
lush greenery that would
cease to exist
without it.
"But how long will that darkness last?"
he foolishly asks himself.
Nevertheless,
here you are.
Just like the cloud will surely bring rain,
he has no choice but to face
you.
  Change.

Change seems to occur in small bursts,
consistently,
over time,
without thought.
She runs toward it constantly,
yet the more it evades her.
It only occurs when in a standstill,
appreciating all that life brings
and respecting the process.
Only in the moment
will she finally meet it.
        The irony.

She used to present her edited self to you
after you didn't accept her.
But that only left her with someone
she couldn't recognize.
She should've removed you from her life
before she lost herself.
Now she's attempting to undo it all:
   Ctrl-Z.

Today, he said no
to his inner demons.
He said no
to their demands.
He said no
to their expectations
and
breathed.
And
breathed.
And
breathed.
　　　Attempting to stay grounded.

There's a faint light,
a glimmer of hope.
Would she be foolish
if she were to run toward it?
A glimpse of the first sparkle returning to her eye.

Relief washes over him.
Was facing his fears
always this easy?
        D-day.

Each breath is starting to become
easier.
Each day is starting to become
bearable.
She stands in her bleak, dark room
and opens the curtains,
inviting the warmth of the sun
in.

     A few days after.

His heart is longing for
something that it doesn't
know...
　　　yet.

The sun has risen;
the day has begun.
Will it be a new beginning?
The sun has risen;
the unknown is to happen.
Curiosity consumes her.
So, she rises with the sun,
hoping her curiosity
will lead her to a new
                    beginning.

Chapter 4
LOSS

I wish to rewind time,
to be with those whom I love
one last time,
and to erase those moments
I hated most.
    I miss you, Daddy.

i was five years old when i first
met the sea.
"Cold, salty, deep."
That's how i described it to my father
as he stood behind me.
Despite its intimidating body,
its waves were slow and inviting,
compelling me to trust it.
The tide began grazing closer
to where i stood.
With both small hands,
i gathered my dress
and cautiously tiptoed toward
the obscure line dividing the sea from the sand.
Right foot,
          left foot.
Right foot,
          left foot.
My father following at my heels.
At that moment,
i felt most brave.
Suddenly, a strange sensation climbed my spine
column by column
as the strength of the wave
swallowed my small figure.
My father pulled me into his strong arms,
guarding,
safe.

That was eighteen years ago.
The sea still intrigues me,
though its waves are no longer inviting
as they crash into one another.
Some days, i attempt to venture out
before coming to a stop,
feeling the heavy absence of my father's footsteps
preventing me from continuing.
      Cemented in the sand.

Dear Daddy,
You were there for each of my milestones.
Your tears abundant and moving every heartless
person observing your love for me.
You cried at every opportunity.
Now, it's time for me to do the same.
I caressed your cold head
for the last time that day,
decorating your face with my salty raindrops,
hoping it'll give life to you once more.
And so, I continue to cry
and cry
and cry.
Out of happiness that you're no longer suffering.
Out of sadness that you're no longer present.
And now, as I write this, it rains
and rains
and rains.
And I wonder if the earth that used to carry
your weight as you tread its paths
may be grieving you too.
        No light in sight.

My heart overflows with
a combination of nostalgia and remorse,
remembering not a specific moment
but remembering it all.

I breathe in,
>   remembering the little girl who used to ride in her
>   daddy's car
>   after the early morning prayer, wrapping her cold
>   fingers around a cup of hot chocolate.

I breathe out,
>   remembering the coldness of her father's palms as he
>   lay lifeless, wrapped in white.

Feeling it all,
over and over.

I breathe in,
>   feeling my daddy's overwhelming happiness on my
>   wedding day as he kissed my forehead.

I breathe out,
>   feeling an overbearing sadness wrap me like a cloak
>   as I tend to my responsibilities,
>   unable to visit my father.

My heart can't help but weep longingly,
regretful I couldn't be with him
during his last moments.
>   A year later.

My palms softened
after I loosened my grip
on the things I couldn't
control.
Sometimes, growth
requires letting go.
Forgiving myself for all those moments.

I go to the places we used to visit,
expecting to find traces of you.
But just like the sea removes the prints in the sand,
time has removed proof of your existence.
Despite it all,
you remain alive within me.
I will remember you
                              eternally.

Two snowflakes dancing elegantly in the air
must eventually meet the ground.
You will be my winter's day,
and each snowflake I see
sparkling in a bed of snow
will remind me of the laughter,
the tears,
and the memories
we made during our flight.
    We were destined to part, but I will always love you.

Chapter 5
CLOSURE

The head of the table was reserved
for him.
She conceded to the side chair,
quiet and forgiving.
But now,
the side chair became the head of the table,
a place he could not keep.
Her shoulders are heavy.
Still,
she straightens her back.
		The slave now becomes the master.

He was never the person
she wanted him to be.
Instead, he was everything
she wanted to be.
She couldn't stand it.
So, she tried to pull him down,
but she forgot he was the sun,
made to rise after every fall.
Sunrise.

She didn't realize the power
her words held
until she saw the lengths
some would go
to silence her.
    She can smell their fear.

She hammered his resolve
like a metalsmith
and dipped him in fire,
only to find him
stronger and more precious
than before.
      Golden.

Her parents worked too hard
to teach her how to stand up tall
not to have the likes of him
treat her like a cane.
    She wasn't meant to carry his weight.

If it weren't for her,
he wouldn't have awakened
the courage that was dormant
with him.
     Cup half full.

She was a diamond,
but his eyes still wandered
after coal.

    Fool's gold.

She was a fool
in love,
just not with the one
sharing her bed.
And that was not his fault.
     Her loss.

Choosing herself meant
challenging generations
of learned indifference
where the woman
is taught to expect nothing
and endure everything.
        Rewriting her future.

He hopes that she's able
to see the pain
she put him through
so that she can seek
the help that she needs.
He hopes that she changes her ways
so that no one ever breaks
by her hands again.
He hopes that her cold heart
bleeds warmth
once more.
      Last wish.

Love should not hurt.
Love should not cause pain.
Love should not make you doubt yourself.
If it does,
that is not love.
That is abuse.
    Words of advice.

I'm sorry you were too much
for them.
I'm sorry your love was too warm
for them.
I'm sorry your forgiveness was too suffocating
for them.
I'm sorry your accomplishments were too
grand for them.
I'm sorry your strength was too intimidating
for them.
I'm sorry that their velvety palms were not capable
of grasping all the human that you are.
I'm sorry that they will come to know
that you were never too much,
but they were not enough.
It'll be too late by then.
      End scene.

Chapter 6
REBIRTH

The fog is beginning to lift.
His mind is beginning to clear;
his heart is beginning to lighten.
Is this what he has been waiting for?
The calm after the storm.

She cups her hands together,
preparing for all the blessings
she's been long
                awaiting.

He tried to not depend on anyone,
but he realized
that even the earth
needs to be cared for
in order to grow.
　　　　Maturation.

She wanders through the paths
in her backyard,
hoping to stumble across
inspiration.
Little did she know
that it was within her
all along.
        She is home.

Who is God?
He knew Him very well.
But he forgot about Him for a while
out of anger,
out of doubt.
It's been a while,
but he'd like to remember Him
again.
      Repentance.

There are times where she'd like to erase
all that is her
and start over with a fresh canvas,
painting an image of the person she is now,
the person she wants to be.
She's so different from the naïve,
young girl she once was.
Now,
she doesn't know who she is—
she doesn't know what she is.
But she's content with that.
She'll figure it out one day.
Until then,
she'll continue to paint with all the colors
that appeal to her naked eye.
She'll embrace all the curved and crooked lines,
she'll combine the dark and bright colors
fearlessly,
and she'll be pleased with the results,
regardless of what others say.
She'll name it a
                    masterpiece.

Laughter didn't exist
in his world for a long time,
but now,
he hears it all around him.
        Yellow.

Hands envelop her,
tightening together.
She stands in the middle of them all,
guarded.
Safe.
Grateful.
      Support.

The sun has set;
the waves have calmed.
The tides have drawn in,
removing all traces of their footprints.
The comfort of the night has finally arrived.
They finally make their way to the obscure line that separates
the sand from the sea,
allowing it to reach the depths of their souls.
Come dawn,
they'll journey out once more.
As for now,
they remain.
       A new beginning.

Epilogue
YOU

My love,
the clay we were created from
was meant to break
and be remolded
and break
and be remolded.
    Repeat.

You were created
with a purpose.
Your presence
was not haphazard.
Everything about you
is unique.
Don't ever allow
anyone to treat you
as anything less
than the extraordinary
being you are.
                With love.

Dear you,
I've been sent to
teach you the things
happiness could not.
So please,
let me in.
Allow me to dance in the
red rivers running
beneath your skin.
I promise I won't stay for long.
Once I've etched the lessons
into the deepest
parts of your being,
we will part ways.
And if you see me later
from a distance,
remember the words
I had scribed,
and run the other way.
            Sincerely, pain.

And in the end,
you knew all the
I love you's in the world
would mean nothing
if it didn't surpass their tongue.
  Fake love.

You desired to be loved
so obsessively
that you accepted
all the blame,
endured all the pain,
while trying to put out
their flame,
hoping that doing so
would bring you their
warmth afterward.
But it didn't.
You only burned.
        Ashes is all that you will gain.

If you're still wondering why
they did what they had done,
you're still clinging
on to the idea that they
didn't mean to hurt you.
And that will cause
you to accept whatever half-hearted
excuse they conjure up.
But don't fall for it;
they meant to hurt you.
Accept it before they take advantage
of your kindness
again.
        History repeats itself.

Some bridges
are better burned
than crossed.
       Set it aflame.

Holding on to them
was like holding on to
water—
          impossible.

You allowed your identity
and value
to be tied to their presence,
and that was your biggest mistake.
Lesson learned.

Listen to your body:
the way your breath catches,
the way your heart races anxiously,
the way your fingers become clammy,
the way your eyes become wide.
Your body is signaling you to run.
Yet there you stand,
welcoming their embrace
before they feast.
      Dinner.

They say good women
are for good men,
and good men
are for good women,
as if good people
can't cause
or experience pain.
As if being a good person
will exempt you from
the trials and tribulations
of this life.
I'm sorry to say
that's not the case.
            Goodness is not a shield.

& good people are merely
caves of darkness
illuminated by the single flame
of a candle,
vulnerable to the breeze
that blows.
    Goodness is fragile.

Sometimes, you need
to experience
a bad relationship
in order to appreciate
the ultimately good one.
        Life lessons.

Within you lies
the medicine to your pain.
Within you lies
the answers to your questions.
Within you lies
the certainty to your doubt.
Within you lies
abundance.
Sometimes, you just need
someone else to
voice it for you.
         You are whole.

I see the storm
brewing within you.
I see the traditions
of your people weighing as boulders
atop your tired shoulders,
bending your spine into prostration.
And yet,
I see a single spark of fire
blazing,
contained within your eye.
I see you holding on.
Before you realize it,
the storm will give way
to a thunder so strong
it will shake the very depths
of your soul
and unleash that fire
that you're so desperately trying to control.
I see it all within you.
I just wish you could see it, too.

      I am you.

If you continue to listen
to the opinions of others,
you will drown in a pool
of words that were intended
as life jackets.
        Trust yourself.

Losing a loved one
comes with a plethora of regrets,
what-ifs,
and a debilitating pain
that feels endless.
But, just as every chapter must come to an end,
so will the regrets.
So will the what-ifs.
But the pain will always remain,
just watered down enough to continue living.
       Forever embedded.

You will never
be able to rewind time,
so stop allowing
yesterday to exist,
and make space
for today.
        Forgive yourself.

As long as your heart
continues to beat,
you have another opportunity
to change your life.
      Good things come to those who do.

There's so much beauty
in the rain.
If only you could
see past the clouds.
      Rainbow.

Be the flower
that finds a way
to flourish between
the cracks in the pavement.
        Optimism.

Don't allow your situation
or circumstance to define you;
rather, allow it to be a part of you.
If it defines you,
then that's all that you are,
all that you'll ever amount to.
But if it's a part of you,
then it's just a small piece
of the puzzle that makes up
the beautiful image
that is you.
Bigger picture.

& the next time
you look into the mirror,
say to those broken eyes,
"I'm proud of you
for fighting to see
despite it all."
Mantra one.

& the next time
you sit with yourself,
say, "I promise to listen
to your silence,
even when it becomes
deafening,
for those are the moments
when you say the most."
        Mantra two.

& the next time
you're hiding beneath the covers,
say, "I promise to love you
even on the days you hate
the color brown,
for those are the days
you need it most."
Mantra three.

There are times when life
is like spilled milk;
a misfortune will occur
suddenly,
unexpectedly,
and completely
out of your control.
Know,
it is okay to cry.
Your tears may be
enough to fill the sea
or as miniscule as a few drops,
but the milk will remain
a pearly white puddle at your feet.
So, my love,
when you are *ready*,
wipe your tears,
pull up your boots, and
jump.
   Splash onward.

Life is a train;
some people get on and off
at different times.
Some will accompany you
for a short while,
and some will stay a little longer,
depending on where your headed.
Some of the people on board
will anger you with their ways;
some will bring you a moment of joy
with their laughter,
and some will bring you peace
with their stillness.
Each meeting is purposeful.
Their boarding will teach you something;
their departure will teach you something,
and even their anger will teach you something.
But don't get caught up in the
hustle and bustle of the train
that you forget to enjoy the ride
to where you're destined.
The sweetness is in the journey.

To the one reading the words scribed on my heart,
to the one enduring a similar fate,
and to the one in search of a light on their darkest days:
know,
it'll all come to pass.

Three things:

Firstly,
during this entire process,
I've learned to embrace
all the emotions—
the anger,
the sadness,
and even the regret—
for each emotion
has a purpose
that you will come to fear, hate,
and lastly, appreciate.

Secondly,
pain loves to be coddled,
constantly carried by its victim,
nursed at every cry,
and never to be forgotten.

It provokes sleepless nights
and worry-filled days,
demanding attention at every possible
moment.

During this time,
realize that pain is universal—
not related to a specific people
but inevitably carried
in the blood of the past,
present,
and future generations.
You are not alone.

And lastly,
when you deal with someone else's pain,
you won't be left alone with your own.
Opening your heart to the pain of others
will allow seeds of gratitude to be planted
in between the broken pieces of your heart.
So, continue to water those seeds,
and observe how your heart
begins to heal—
a garden of flowers replacing
the painful pieces of your memory.

So, to the one reading the words scribed on my heart,
to the one enduring a similar fate,
and to the one in search of a light on their darkest days:
know,
it'll all come to pass.
You will remain.
I promise.

About the Author

Aisha is a 23-year-old Registered Respiratory Therapist and single mother to a 3.5-year-old boy with autism. Aisha resides in Edmonton, Alberta, where she practices Respiratory Therapy and enjoys spending her spare time in the kitchen alongside her son, creating food recipes for her blog www.kitchenkonfessions.ca. You can also find more of Aisha's poetry and journey to healing on her Instagram page @aishamali_.

CPSIA information can be obtained
at www.ICGtesting.com
Printed in the USA
BVHW082140040220
571444BV00001B/114